Notes

from the

Coffee Table

reflective moments from when things change.

William S. Peters, Sr.

inner Child Press, ltd.

Credits

Author

William S. Peters, Sr.

Cover Design

'just bill'

Foreword

Janet P. Caldwell

Editor

Janet P. Caldwell

Cover Photograph

Steven Heap

123RF.com

General Information

Notes from the Coffee Table

reflective moments from when things change

William S. Peters, Sr.

1st Edition : 2013

Publisher Information

1st Edition : Inner Child Press :
intouch@innerchildpress.com
www.innerchildpress.com

LOC : 1-941737221

ISBN-13 : 978-0615826370
ISBN-10 : 0615826377

$ 21.95

Dedication

for all those who must face change . . .

it is inevitable

however . . .

you are not alone.

Foreword

In this book, *Notes from the Coffee Table,* We, the reader will notice what is all too familiar with most of us and that is blaming others for our illusion of pain. Bill shows us the way to take our lives into our own hands and not a soul can do it except you, me and us. Self examination and reflections from a man, that is so private about the relationships that he has experienced are astounding. In this realm he includes love, loss, passion . . . while maintaining the beauty within and encouraging us to remove the masks of un-authenticity.

I was pleasantly surprised that he shared so much. It is raw, no candy coating to be found, though there is always love in the searching. I am One, who is intimately involved with this man, and I must say that I am Blessed to know him. Even more so, that the strong mask has been removed and we see the blood spilling, we all bleed, don't we ? We also see the Warrior in action and a Warrior he is, fighting for his freedom to simply *Be* without judgment.

He is not only a Warrior but a Conscious One and strives for the good of the Whole. Self examination can be a brutal exercise for some. Just look in the Spiritual mirror. It is a challenge for so many. Bill has shown us by example it is necessary to *Know* ourselves first and to love ourselves, in order to make a change that will make a positive difference in our lives and those of others.

I have enjoyed working with him on this manuscript and many times the tears fell. However, it has propelled me to take a step back, observe *my own* perceptions / perspectives, and to not engage on an emotional level while making my own changes. *Notes from the Coffee Table* will definitely show another side to this Giant of a Man, and cause you to wonder how he made it through all of the loss. We are all One, if he can, so can you. He wraps it up with poems of tenderness that we all vie to experience. It has been my honor to be a part of his journey.

I encourage you to take a trip with the man Himself on this drive called "crazy little thing called love." or as it is titled, *Notes from the Coffee Table*. Grab your box of tissues and join me for the ride of your life. Did I say page turner? It must have been in my mind after reading and editing this blow your mind manuscript. Enjoy, I did.

Janet P. Caldwell / Author

a cup of Coffee

a Cigarette

a Pen and Pad

is the start of a good day.

Preface

Notes from the Coffee Table appeared at my doorstep of consciousness unexpectantly. Being a Writer / Poet, i pride myself on my listening abilities. I love being observant, hoping to gather some inspiration to continue expressing, not only myself from my experiential perspectives, but in hopes to write something that is more far reaching than the "*Me*". I believe *Notes from the Coffee Table* is just that type of Creative Offering.

Everyone experiences *Change*. Some changes are prolific and some are subtle. When life calls for us to experience more dramatic changes such as exemplified by way of Relationship, Death and a few other potential *Life Altering* situations, we become introspective. In *Notes from the Coffee Table* i was able to tap into my own experiences of having a Life Mate / Wife transition as well as having to go through the ending of other meaningful relationships. Every time i have found myself surrounded with a myriad of Questions, Thoughts and Emotions. Here in *Notes from the Coffee Table,* i am sharing such introspective, retrospective and circumspective pondering. Most of us either have or will experience this at times in our life.

My objective and intent is but to perhaps touch something in the reader that is common to us all. In that, hopefully someone will be able to take the short cut toward self reconciliation.

Blessed Be

bill

Table of Contents

The Notes

Table of Contents . . . *continued*

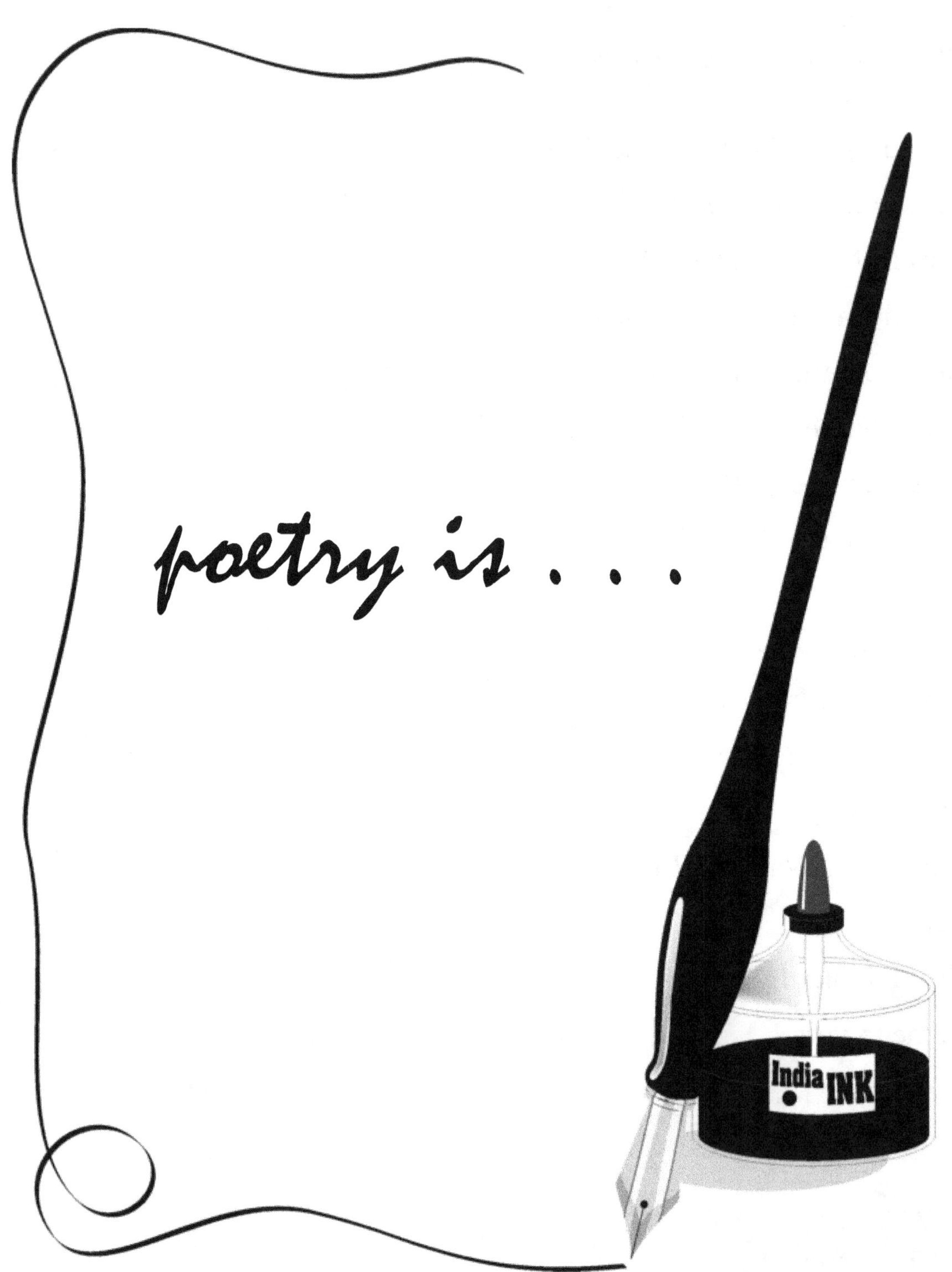
poetry is . . .
India INK

the more time i take to look at my self
the more i can clearly see
that i am so much more
than what i believe that i am.

william s. peters, sr.

William S. Peters, Sr.

Notes

from the

Coffee Table

reflective moments from when things change.

William S. Peters, Sr.

inner Child Press, ltd.

self contemplation
is the sweetest of gifts.

a Note on the Coffee Table

i woke up this morning
yawning
as usual
with the dawning Light

The bright Sun was beaming
through our window
making the call
to begin the tasks of the day

i rolled over
to where my Love
my Lover
should have been
and she was not there

i thought nothing of it
perhaps she was in the Bathroom
or the Kitchen
making ready
to do her daily thing
. . . Love me
loving me
and me loving her

i did detect the aroma
of Coffee wafting
through the air
and my face wrinkled
with an expectation
of seeing her again
her face
as i kissed her lips
and embraced her hips
as i drew her into my space

i held that vision
of we two
in the kitchen
and that first sip of Coffee
and a Cigarette

i went to the bathroom
brushed my teeth
washed my face
and i took a leak
flushed the toilet
and exited
and made my way
to where she would be
the Kitchen

My love, my Lover
was no where to be found
but i did smell those fresh grounds
steaming
as the Sun was beaming
through our Kitchen window

i wondered
where has my Love gone

i poured my self a cup
doctored it with
Sugar and Cream
as the steam
tickled my nostrils
i took a sip
lit me a cigarette
and puffed
inhaled
and sighed

i went to the Living Room
the room where we lived out
most of our days together

i sat on the couch
grabbed the Daily News
and i noticed
a neatly folded paper
sitting there waiting
for me
to investigate
what it was
and what it may have to say

i started to dismiss it
but i could not resist it
so i picked it up
and this is
what it said

My Dear Love

This morning i have awakened before you
instead of with you.

I have missed out on
our early morning greetings
and our session of love
but i did make you some
fresh coffee.

You are now more than likely
sitting on the couch
drinking your coffee
and reading this note
my heartfelt attempts
to share with you
my heart felt feelings

Note from the Coffee Table

As much as i would love
to be with you
in these cherishable moments
of a new day
our new day
i am not
for i am embracing a new way
of my own.

Yes, i have awakened
this day

i have come to an Epiphanic realization
that i want more
i will not be forsaking
the potentials
of what i may become

i want more
things
to explore
why my Soul no longer sings
of it's joy
during our routinous rehearsals
of the same old songs
we both know
all too well

i long to be young again
in love like a young school girl
on her first date
and of late
all i can think of
is possibilities
of what else i may be missing

life is short
this is what i have seen

this is not to say
i do not love you
for i do
deeper than i have ever loved another
and you gave it back to me
more than i have ever been loved
before

but it is you who opened that door
that spoke to me
awoke me
and showed me
a realm
where i am at the helm
of my life's ship,
and i thank you
truly i do

but today i have awakened
and i saw the Sunshine
yes, the same old Sun
we see every day
and i wanted to go out
and play
in the fields of life
and feel the rife
of a Joy
i have yet to experience
and i know you do
understand

you will always be my man
and if you are there
when i return
if i choose to return
i will share with you
what i have discovered
about me
and then perhaps
we can uncover
a greater possibility

of what we may become
as One Love

and in closing
i am supposing
that there is a smile in your heart
as i impart to you
what my soul is saying
and speaking to me

and finally . . . i would like to
Thank you for reading this
Note on the Coffee Table

i love you

a note for you . . . i hope you "Get It" . . . get it ?

My Love,

i will not lament
and allow the energy of my confusion
and surprise
to suppress your potential joy

the best i may offer unto you
and life
is a blessing
of God Speed
and a Good Journey
as you wander in your wonder
seeking that which you always had
within you

i do understand your penchant to know
for all Souls should be graced
by the presence
and light
of the actualization
of their greater selves

that truly is a blessing
of the highest order

i shall make no promises
to be idle
and allow my soul to rust
in the trust
that you may return
for i too
do not wish to pick up old things
or sing old songs
for i too long for more
than what i have experienced
in my life thus far

Note from the Coffee Table

i just thought it would be with you

there is no fault
to be had
and our love was far more
than a fad
it was
and is
still valid
for i gave you my heart
as you did for me

so in the end
or should i say
in the new beginning
be that what you wish to be
for you have always been free
to do that

smile at your self
and with your self
in your life path
with each foot step
mile after mile
and the world does smile
with you

so with this
until maybe then
i bid you adieu
it is nice having loved you

and
i love you still

notes from the Coffee Table # 3

Here i sit

here i sit
contemplating the effects
of change
that has come into our lives

you have chosen a new path
and left me at a juncture
where i too must
decide my direction
and press on

last night
as i lay my head
upon my pillow
i could not help but feel
the silence
the solitude
that such an empty bed
evokes

i have become so accustomed
to the touching
the caresses
the strokes
of each other's consciousness
because we were present
but you are not here
save for the haunting
daunting
flaunting memories
of what used to be

i found myself indulging
in the divulging
that i too have dwelled
perhaps too much
in that void
of what may be
that chasm
of the expectant me
who has went to sleep

yes i too took you
took us
for granted

i could go on
sharing in this note
i now write
about my struggles last night
that lasted to the dawn
of a new day
but it did not feel so new
and i knew
it was because you
were not there

the Sun did greet me
in spite of me
and what i may have thought
or been thinking
as it was winking at me
between the slats
of the blinds

i forgot to draw them closed
as i have now closed a portion of my heart
which is no longer open
to experience
my perceived hurt
in your absence

yes i am now absent
from the classroom
where i thought
i have come to learn
of my authenticity
which i implicitly
pursued

but what i was pursuing
was my visions
my thoughts
my dreams

and though it may seem
that they were once One
i now know this was not
an ultimate truth
nor a sustaining reality
devoid of pain

yes, now as i examine
the insanity of my falsehood
which i embraced
with a certainty
i must confess,
for i now see
the inanity
of what we men
come to believe
if no one stirs
the conscious stew
we are cooking

but when it is all said and done
i will deliberately come undone
that i may remake my self
mold my self
without an exacerbescence
that only i can conjure

Note from the Coffee Table

so for as sure
as i sit here in reflection
introspectively inspecting
with retrospection
at the intersection of change
correction is not what i need
nor seek

i just wish to peek
at my self
and the rock that is missing
from my life
that i thought was you

so now, here i sit
at the Coffee Table of my life
writing another Note
in consternation
a compilation of me
looking at me again

these are my Notes from the Coffee Table

notes from the Coffee Table # 4

here i sit at the Coffee Table
of my consciousness
pondering
examining
inspecting
the possibilities
of the possibilities

i am calling them back
in to the realm of my “Be”ing-ness
which is right here
right now . . .
this frozen moment
where a certain stillness
prevails

some are old
some are new
some i have known
some i once knew
and some just are

what path shall life
present to me ?
will i see the present
it presents
to my presence,
or shall i shuffle it aside
because it challenges me
and calls for a commitment
i am not ready to ascribe
in this moment
of introspection ?

life has proven once again
that it is always
evolving
while i,
yes i,

Note from the Coffee Table

many times get stuck
telling my self i am
solving problems
that i have created
with my limited perspectives

i find that
i too am evolving
to greater expressions
where boundaries
appear silly at best

perhaps that is the test
of all souls
to see if we will be contained
stained
profaned
by the illusory aspects
of this existence
which allows us to be comfortably deluded
because there are so many
just like me
or at least just like i see my self

some times the questions
become heavy
and i must put them down
for like the cosmic clown
i have demonstrated an ability
to be so proficient at
the inane

i realize
this is the time to laugh
so i laugh at me
at you
at life
at God
for He does too
have a seemingly sick
sense of humor

from my vantage point
how about you

when i consider the trials
and tribulations
and the miles along the road
i have traveled
and the view
i have been blessed to encounter,
i must simply say
thank you i guess
for that seems to me to be
the sensible way of approaching it all

and though there may never be any full
reconciliation
i am Okay with that
for in between the doubts of it all
i can most certainly conjure up
a few Mustard Seeds of faith
and let go of the unseen
for i do get to verify it's mystique
as i peek blindly
at the meaning of it all

so in summation
again i admit
reconciliation would be nice
and perhaps that is what i am exercising,
my right to question
ponder
inspect
examine
and determine perhaps
as i extricate such things
for the consideration
of some distant part of me
which resides in that void
i am attempting to discover
in my notes from the Coffee Table

notes from the Coffee Table # 5

here i sit once again,
this time speaking with my best friend
ME !

yes i am having a conversation
with my God
and my God
is he judgmental

in surveying the many paths
i have traveled
the many perfectly working apparatuses
in my life
i have unraveled
i can not help but smile at my self

there is nothing wrong
with a little levity
is there ?
it does wonders
with distracting me from my fears
that i often voice
about life
and the seemingly limited choices
i offer my self

and the hypocrisy of it all
i tell my self
"All things are possible"
though i have not found my way
to that cupboard as of yet

yes many times
or is it all times
we are the ones
that shun our blessings
while confessing to the unknown
about our perceived weaknesses
asking for help

and Soul-utions
we already possess

Greed ?

i think God does not listen to that nonsense
because His Omniessence knows
that we are just like Him or Her
whichever you prefer

Omnipotent ~ Omniscient ~ Omnipresent

he knows that we are truly strong
and have been all along
but we did not want to face the responsibility
so we are drawn to some
false fragility
and we want others to join us

hey . . .let's have a party
since we are all here

when will i learn to trust
in the Gifts i already possess
instead of questing
for more illusions
that i can appear normal
by the LOWER standards of expression

another "shake my head" moment

i like you have often asked
"why am i here ?"
"what is it i am meant to do?"
only to be left in the silence
where my own rationale
must fill the void

sometimes that works for me
but . . .
yes, i do get annoyed
with that God Guy in me
don't you
maybe a little ?

but i must be careful
in how i say that
and where and to whom
or the world will nail me to a Cross
or hang me from a Tree
for exercising Blasphemy
which is my right . . . of course
but the World of them there other folks
don't see it that way

but in the end
i realize
i do not control
what their psychic eyes
tell them
and like usual
i am okay with that
even through the struggle

ahhhhh . . . Good Coffee

Notes from the Coffee Table

notes from the Coffee Table # 6

yes, here i sit
at the Coffee Table once again

it is another day
just like the other day
just me, myself and i
contemplating what to write about
that may be truthful in my examination
of my life
that i now am experiencing
without you

Somehow i feel i am still fixated
on you
and there are a few things
i have yet to work out
a few things left
unsaid
in my head
my spirit
my heart
that i wish to impart
to you
even though
you are not here

so i am addressing this to you

perhaps some day you may read this
but i must get it out of me
i just must . . . and thus

Dear Love,

since you have left me
with this empty Couch
empty Bed
empty Kitchen
empty Heart

empty Life
i find that i have much work to do
in filling the
empty space
you have left behind

is life kind
that fate
should extricate you
from my physical existence
where the only consistence
of your presence
is in my memories

i told my self
i would not lament
for i thought i was strong
and tears were not meant
for me

but now as i write
my eyes are filled
with moist salted remnants
that seek to fill my life
in lieu of the smiles
we once shared

yes . . . tears
and some fears
of what tomorrow may bring

this silence that prevails
about me
permeating my day
my thoughts of it
and all the possible shit
one could ever think of
about a love lost
is costing me
much energy
i would rather spend

loving you
as we used to do

but i know those times have now passed
and now i find my self
coming to believe
that nothing good does last
and this has painted my heart's hopes
with dismal colors
of Dark Blues, Purples and Grays

what can one say ?

this note may appear painful
and i guess to some degree it is
but in truth
i am trying my best
to get you out of me
even if it is but for
a moment
that i may find some peace

and in the end
you are not here
to share these thoughts with

so here i sit
again
writing . . .
notes from the Coffee Table

notes from the Coffee Table # 7

again, yes again
here i am in my own
little temporary Temple of Solace
and Reflection
a bundle of Mind stuff
stuck in the introspection
attempting to figure out
where i am
what i am going through
and how may i reconcile
this storm i feel is impending
in my emotions
and other expressions
of self

there is something looming about
ushering a movement
to doubt my self
Me
and whether i am truly
in control

sure, they tell me
"Life is as i see it"
but heretofore
what i have seen
is losing it's validity
as i evaluate the absurdity
of what i thought to be true

there are times
i am OK with me
and times i feel so blind
i just can not see
ME !!!!

this is one of those times
where i do so need to define
something
and hope that it is meaningful
yes, meaningful enough
to stick around for a minute . . .
a very long minute.
you know . . .
like that minute where the eternal
glimpses at it's self

it is not that i am not at peace
yes, i can cease this type of discourse
and of course
perspective
is my elective
to exercise
as i choose

but somehow
it does so resemble
the semblance
of another delusion
which i have become quite adept
and adroit
in creating
that i may move on . .
mind you, with the burden
of unanswered questions
being dragged into my momentous future

such a nice word "Peace" is
as is Happiness
but i have only seen them
in their brevity
as they bring forth a levity
to my life i strive for
that they may become permanent guests
in my house

what i now ask
for the tasks of my life
do endure
in their amiss-ness

there are decisions
always to be made
about this or that
and yes, i do understand
i can
decide to ‘not’ choose
but what would that resolve ?

it seems that every time i lace up
my boots
somehow
the knots of security
come undone
i trip
and i become
the knotted one
within
again and again

with a certainty
i have prayed
fervently
unceasingly

and this, is but another sequestering
of the greater of all things
to finally speak
with some audibleness
that i can be affirmed
that i am hearing it all correctly
i need this directly
you know

within the silence
the only aspect of any value
still remains this smile of mine
for the tears do serve purpose
time and time again
but the smiles
yes, the smiles
are so much more
and i embrace them
in their scarcity

they are a joy filled experience
as is recording such meandrous examinations
of this consciousness
so i guess
i must say
i am blessed !

i am blessed to have this voice
for me, for all that i care for
dare for
which visits from time to time
as i sit
writing this note
from my Coffee Table.

Notes from the Coffee Table

notes from the Coffee Table # 8

it would seem that the journey
of reconciliation
with Self
with God
is another "Never Ending Story"

again here i am reflecting
on the time i have spent
with me
since you went away

i am not complaining
for what good would it provide
nor will i hide
behind the curtains of excuses

i can not say that i am troubled
to any great degree
i am just examining life
. . . me
and it's meaning
whenever i can find some

through my writings
i exact
as i sit here
with a cup of Coffee
a Cigarette
there are small measures
of reflective sweetness
i get to taste
from time to time
and i am thankful

today again
the Sun did shine
not only for me
but the world
of which i now understand
i am a part of
even though you have
parted ways
with me

i have not yet become comfortable enough
to invite a possible suitable substitute
in lieu of your company,
your presence
in my heart
for that is all they would be
a temporary fix
to an issue
i have yet to comprehend
how to decode

sometimes i am burdened
by the load
the need for clarity
life offers me

and because i can not carry it
i tarry not under its weight
i just sit it down upon paper
and wait for the answers
that never seem to come
as i thought they would
or should

i now wonder
if i could change things
would i
should i
and all i come up with is smiles
about the possibilities
as to how things would appear now
especially knowing what i now do
about me
about you

each day i think i am seeing more of me
and i am coming to a point
of becoming to like
this space
that is not as empty
as it once seemed
when you first left

i mean
my dreams have expanded
to include different textures
and colors
and songs
and i am dancing again
to strange new melodies
i some how feel
i faintly remember
from so long ago

actually, life is wonderful . . .
not because you are gone,
but what your departure
brought to me

somehow, these moments do confirm
something i never thought of before
and that is
if Karmic Law is as valid
as i believe it to be
then i was not as bad
as i saw my self
when you first went away

and this day
as i sit and record these thoughts
these writings
i have decided to rejoice
for i still live
and to the world i give
my most cherished reflections
in my
Notes from the Coffee Table

notes from the Coffee Table # 9

Dear God, this note is for you

God, you have seen me,
heard me and perhaps listened in
as i have been examining my life
and its various aspects

i have prayed so much,
and you know it . . . don't you ?

funny thing God,
i thought prayers were answered
or that is what i thought them to be for

but it seemed like
you never spoke to me
or perhaps you just whispered
and i did not hear you
because i was too busy
thinking about things
life things

as you may well know
some days have been a struggle
other days . . . i get by
but it really would be so nice
if we could have a 1 on 1
you and i

each day is a struggle
to remain positive
hopeful
and it would be helpful
if you would just
give me a sign

i really don't mind
if you do not have time
to answer
all of my request
as i sequester you
and the providence of comfort
only you can deliver

tonight again
i know the sheets
will be cold
and the bed empty
and i am not so sure
i would want a warm body
next to me
just for the sake
of company,
but it would be nice
if i could find some peace
in the sea of all this loneliness

so God,
perhaps i do not understand
your ways
and the plan you have
for my days
but i do so wish
you would say something
any thing
that could help me make it through
to
another day
of writing these
Notes from the Coffee Table

notes from the Coffee Table # 10

O K
it's been 2 weeks
since you have been gone
and like they say
the beat goes on

yes, there were times
i doubted
i even screamed
shouted
at the moon
praying you would return
soon
as the tears streamed
down my face

the space you left behind
is still empty
except for the memories,
but that's a good empty
if you know what i mean

i mean like
for the first time
in a long time
i am seeing me
and the myriad of possibilities
that life now presents
as a present
that i am now learning how
to unwrap

right now, life
may appear to be
in a state of flux
and i know
that i can handle it
... at least
that is how i feel
and what i tell my self
in this moment

no more crutches to lean on
now that you are gone

today is a good day
to die . . .to live
and in my current
reconciliatory perspectives
i am choosing to give
to life
all of me
all of the time

well, at least
that is my intent

so here i sit
once again
at what used to be
"our" Coffee Table
writing these notes,
sharing my life examinations
and my "evolutionary" thoughts
as i am "awakening"

Note from the Coffee Table

i am de-ensnaring my self
from my past
and the things i once bought in to
as if the Fairy Tale would last

Note : it does you know
once we acknowledge
that we grow
continually
with no affinity to
what we have been
going through
or what is to come

i wonder as i ponder
and i ponder in my wonder
in these humble Notes from the Coffee Table

notes from the Coffee Table # 11

well here i am
once again
sitting here alone
at the Coffee Table

i usually do no find my self
writing at this time of day
the evening
but since your leaving
i am finding new ways
to express my self
and this is something
i just had to get out

i miss you so terribly

so . . . i made my self
a cup of Coffee
and here i am
on the couch alone
at the Coffee Table
smoking a cigarette
and pondering
once again

i though i had gotten over you
yes, i congratulated my self
because of my "fortitude"
and my "supposed" strength

but today
something happened
it was such a small thing,
but it mocked my world
rocked my world
and moved my mighty mountain

today was laundry day
and i was alright with that
until . . .
i was folding socks
SOCKS !!!!!

i remembered the time
when you showed me
your way
your ways

you being the child of a
Military Man
you did things differently
that us, the rest of the world

you showed me how to lay the socks out
and roll them up
and tuck them in to each other

yes that tuck

well today i cried
over socks
SOCKS !!!!!
that sucks

i do not understand that
i guess it is the memory
of your touch
on my hand

the softness of your hand
as your guided me through
the process
i offered no contest
i could actually feel you

i also remembered the smile
upon your face
that graced the moment
when i got it
and the ensuing kiss
a sweet reward
i shall never forget

i also succinctly recall
how that kiss
led us
to a very special sharing
of bliss that day

God how i miss you
your ways
your touch
and the intimate love
we shared . . . that day

God . . .God . . . God
Why . . .Why . . . Why

Why have you left me at this Coffee Table
alone
with nothing but
this pen
this pad
writing notes ?

notes from the Coffee Table # 12

well here we are
Note # 12

today is a new day
and perhaps i will find
a new way
of living
this day
that will deliver me
away
from this dammed
semi suffering
i have been experiencing
in these reflective moments

each note i write
re-exposes me
to the convolution
i have been experiencing
because my life has been turned
upside down
inside out

i am tired
i feel worn
and my heart feels torn
apart
just because
you chose
to part ways
with the life
we spent so much time
putting together

yes there have been storms
rainy days
but we have shared so many flowers
haven't we ?

we had so many plans
didn't we ?

we could have made it through
couldn't we ?

i wonder why
you did not even take the time
to talk to me
shouldn't we
have talked
instead of you
leaving me
a note on the Coffee Table ?

notes from the Coffee Table # 13

Despair . . .
yes , DESPAIR

i am desperately grasping for air

it seems that i am being choked,
my life is slipping away

they say "this is the day
the Lorde has made
and i shall be happy
and rejoice in it"
and Lorde knows
i am trying

i went on a date last night
i was trying
vying to move on
and i guess i was denying
how much you have affected my life

don't get me wrong
i did have a nice time
and the company was pleasant
but it only served to remind me
how much i missed your presence

you would have been proud of me
perhaps
because i played the part
masterfully . . .

why she even asked me out again
i have to laugh at that one

i feigned having fun
but as the evening waned
the dread crept in
as i faced
going home alone
to that empty house
empty bed
to lay my head
next to no one
except the ghosts
of what used to be

and here all the time
i thought i was happy
and i thought you were too
but you fooled me

maybe you were fooling
your self as well

i now see
clearly
that we both were
telling our selves lies
over the duration of time
we spent together lived together
loved together

i now question
was it truly love at all

was it ?

so now here you are on
to another life path
and in all honesty
i do hope that you have found
what you were seeking

me, i am having the time of my life
peeking
trying to get a glimpse
of who i am
just like you are doing
i guess

well today
was another test
and i think i did not do
as well as i had hoped
yeah, i coped with it

shit !

i guess i am not fairing well
for time away from you
sucks
it smells rotten
every other day
and now here i am
playing games of delusion
with my self
pretending
life is good
while sitting here
filled with despair
gasping for air
as i write this . .
note from the Coffee Table

notes from the Coffee Table # 14

i can not explain why
why do i keep your picture
on the table
beside the bed

maybe this is my way
of keeping a piece of you
close to me
where it counts

i still quite often dream of you
and i
and what may have been
if only

yes, if only

i have asked my self that question
many time
but still there are no answers

if only what

if only you . . . what

if only you never left
but i would not want to have you here
if you were not happy
i guess
but if only

if only i could have been a better man ?

Note from the Coffee Table

wow . . . that's something
that will haunt me
the rest of my days
in every relationship
here after

we shared so many good times
smiles
laughter
tears too
fear too
and little dirty secrets
and
fantasies

and now
you have went away
and the only time i see you
is in the pictures of you
i carry around
in my head
and that picture of you smiling
angelically
lovingly
loving me
next to what once was
our bed

and now all i have is memories
and dreams
of you
and if only . . .
if only

notes from the Coffee Table

notes from the Coffee Table # 15

today i sat on the couch
most of the day
with the telephone
on the table before me

i was in a place
where i knew my hopes
would likely not
be realized
but i could not open my eyes
to the truth

but the truth is
i so wanted that phone to ring
and for it to be you
on the other end

i wanted to hear your voice
yes your voice
that i have not heard
in what now seems to be
aeons

i have been deluding my self
and truthfully
it does serve a purpose
for it gave me a reason
to make it through
but another day

in a previous note
i spoke of my despair
and the labor i experience
in breathing

Note from the Coffee Table

since your leaving
it has been quite a challenge
day by day
hour by hour
minute by minute
moment by moment
and some of those moments
seem to last forever

i have been trying to focus
on the beautiful memories
i can feel them in my heart
along with the pain of
your absence
and i am torn

lately i have been attempting
to distract my self
with tasks and things
and people sometimes too
but it is you
and the memories
that are always waiting for me
in my quiet time

do you remember how
we used to sit around
and do nothing ?
well, now when i sit around
with nothing to do
i succinctly understand
that you were the "some thing"
that made all my nothings
worthwhile

yes, you gave my emptiness
meaning
and still i am filled
by those reflections
those memories
of times we once spent
together
and i cherish them all

i have weathered the storms thus far
and i suppose
i will press on
through this night of my life
to a new dawn,
but damn
this is quite
a long night
of suffering
and the only buffering there is
is that scripture i remember

it is a promise
brighter than any Sun i know
except you being here with me

it said . . .
"weeping may endure for a night,
but joy cometh in the morning"

but for me, this morning
and probably tomorrow as well
i will be telling
what it is my heart
has to say
in these
Notes from the Coffee Table

notes from the Coffee Table # 16

yesterday i went to the park
i decided i wanted to be in touch
with nature

they do say that "*Nature*" heals.
I am not sure if i
needed to be fixed or
if i am broken

i so wanted to fall apart
and perhaps give up.
that is how i feel some days

i sat on the Park Bench
and watched the people going by
the children playing
joyfully unaware
of the pains of the world
the pains of me
or anyone else

they were smiling
uninhibitedly
and i so wanted to smile too
so i faked it
every time
someone would take the time
to look my way

people are amazing
i think

i would imagine many people
who walked on by
have had loved ones
walk out of their lives as well
i imagine that many are
lonely as i am
perhaps more so

as i watched the children
i remembered our plans
for a family
that now lays as wasted thoughts
and dreams
in the refuse containers
of old conversations
and wasted consciousness

it was nice to dream with you
truly
and i do
miss that
those times
when we had no cares for the day
and our dreams drifted away
wherever they may
it was a wonderful time

and here i sit now
reflecting in these writings
of the Notes from the Coffee Table
about the possibilities
we let go
when you chose to go
down another life path
with the children
that could have been

notes from the Coffee Table # 17

angry affirmation

i am tired of wallowing in the mud of anxiety
i am tired of missing you
i am tired of being tired
it is time for me to move on

i did notice when i was angry with you
for dramatically changing our life
i felt so much better
for a while
and then i would feel guilty

some of my thoughts about you
were filthy
and quite unpleasant

but today i am saying
forget you
it is time to do me

you chose to leave
and though i do wish you well
quite frankly
at this moment
"I don't give a damn"

i am not angry any more
but i am learning to let go
even if it is
for but a day
or two

i don't know
if you knew
what you were doing
or how long this has been stewing
in your mind
your heart
your spirit
but i would have love to hear it
some other way
than a note on the Coffee Table

so Damn you
in a nice way
because today
i am getting on
with my life
and it's all about me

notes from the Coffee Table # 18

another day
another struggle

Today it rained
and it flushed my pain
to the surface of my face
as my tears rained down my cheeks
cascading into my heart
awakening memories
of the times we use to spend
together
during those days
those sweet days
when it rained

we would sit right here
where i am now
drinking coffee
talking
sharing dreams
sharing thoughts
giggles and smiles
while listening
to the pitter patter
in between our
incessant chatter

we were so happy then
i thought

but here i am now
alone
with naught
but the reflections
held within
the retrospections
for my inspection
of what used to be

and today is another day
and i struggle
cause i can not see
clearly
from my tears
have blurred my vision

but i so still love you
dearly

and maybe, just maybe
one day
some day
we may
do it again
sharc a day of rain
without this pain
i inanely embrace
as the tears run down my face
dripping
staining
this Note i am writing
from the Coffee Table

notes from the Coffee Table # 19

here i am once again
sitting here at the Coffee Table
contemplating
what it is i wish to say

i do understand
that at some time
i must move on
to a new dawn
a new beginning
and cease dwelling
on you
on our past

my misery lasts
because i am always
thinking about it
this much i do know

but now, it is time for me
to turn over these soils in my garden
pull up the weeds
and sow new seeds
of hope

i have been groping with my self
my emotions
my thoughts
my loneliness
ever since you left

most times i focused on your absence
and i felt a certain emptiness
but i do understand
that some times
i must demand
of myself

to have the courage to create
a new path
for me to travel

yes, my life
that i have become
so accustomed to
has unraveled
but not by my own doing
or was it ?

so many questions
left unanswered
but i must be alright with that
if i am to move on
i must stop holding on
to my self created misery
and delusions

so, this is my affirmation

as soon as i am able
i will quit writing these notes to you
about you
for the only one listening
is me, God and the universe
and that i think is enough
for before i wrote these
Notes from the Coffee Table
they were already inscribed
upon the Tablet of my heart
which is no longer as heavy
as it was
when you first left

notes from the Coffee Table # 20

Yes,
i have cried in my milk
far too damned long

it is time for me
to find
a new song
to sing

i have been sitting here
day after day
letting
allowing my daily ways
to dwell on you
telling you
who happens to not be here
about my ponderings
my wonderings
about you
about me
about life
about God
and my God
it is time for me
to find some peace
don't you think

perhaps now
i am but attempting
to talk my self
into a delusion
but that is ok
for the contusions
you have left within my heart
are healing
as i am spieling
the blood of my illusory anguish
upon these
Notes from the Coffee Table

i shall be healed

notes from the Coffee Table # 21

well today it is raining
the sky is overcast
and gloomy
much like my life has been
off and on
of late

this is a good day
for me to test my resolve

the air is chilly,
but it has been a bit nippy for me
every day
without your warmth

i have to laugh
why ?
because again here i am
sitting at the Coffee Table
doing reflective comparisons
between where i am . . . now
and where i was
once upon a time

maybe i will turn on the Television
and get lost
in the incessant Soul Noise
that streams
continually into my mind
and perhaps i can lose this woe
i feel
and never find it again

you know,
in retrospect
we never did find that picture of us
we misplaced . . .
you know, the one we took
on our first date

i now laugh
at those small forgotten
frantic moments
we shared
when we cared
so deeply
about all the small things
. . . together

yep . . . i am doing it again
remembering
addressing my stressing
over change

but some day i promise
to you
and the ghost of you
and my greater self
that i shall let go
and live

notes from the Coffee Table

notes from the Coffee Table # 22

Today ?
today is a good day for thinking
and i feel that i am no longer sinking
in to that bottomless pit
that void of self
where there are but questions
which are tethered to answers
only i can produce

i have used much of my time
since you left
pondering
wondering
wandering
through the landscapes
of my existence
with a deliberate persistence
to reconcile
and arrest
the conjurings
of my own
ill at ease

Toady . . . yes today
i had a mild revelation
an epiphany of sorts
and i now choose to embrace it
as i face my own
now recreated truths
and i am letting go of the outcome

yes i have heard this before
a dear friend of mine
teaches this
and right now
i am choosing
to trust this

you see
i see
that some people do
come into our lives
for a season
some for a life time
in the empirical sense
and that makes sense to me

but . . . i think
we all bear gifts
for those who can see
life's greater meanings

there are lessons all about us
energies expressing themselves
begging for our consciousness
yet instead of listening
we think without guidance
of the spirit
and create a mess
we only have to later
clean up

well, in letting go of the out come
i am letting go of my Hope
for i have proven
that i can cope
without you

and hope . . . ha !
hope is like
pissing in the wind
and expecting
beautiful waterfalls

so . . .
i shall hope no more
for your return,
for that is not
within the realm of things
i control
only you may direct
your feet
to my door once again
but you must knock

even though my heart's door
is open
and perhaps
i will answer
for i have found
that my need
is not for you
but for my self
as yours is for you
as you so aptly demonstrated
when you withdrew
you "Be"ing-ness
from my space
to seek out your own

had i known before
what i know now
i doubt if i would
have changed a thing

perhaps we could have talked more
perhaps not
but i am so happy for you
truly i am
that you too
are seeking you
and the clarity your soul requires
for the fires
of my quixotic spirit
still burns as well

and as i tell this story
in my Notes from the Coffee Table
i pray that you find your peace
which you seek
within

until then . . .
know that love
never abandons !

notes from the Coffee Table # 23

oh how i loved you
and love you still

over the time since your parting
i have been sorting
out my feelings

yes there was anger and pain
and all the little inane
imaginings
i conjured

i asked my self
countless questions
made somewhat
reconciliatory suggestions
about some one else
in your life

and the truth of the matter
it does not matter
in the least
for my peace
can not be found
in my self induced hauntings
of the falsely passioned wantings
i resurrect
just to justify
the ghosts
that prevails
in your absence

if you were to come to my door
at this moment
i do not know
what my reaction would be
but i should be
in control
shouldn't i

perhaps we would make love
or talk
or maybe i would
turn you away
with the spite
i have experienced
in lieu of the consolation
my heart so desires

but i am ok
for the most part
and my heart
will heal
from the self inflicted wounds
my thoughts
brought forth

and though
today may not be
the best of days
i realize
with wide open eyes
that . .
"this Too Shall Pass"

i wrote a book about that
you know

but in truth
i have had pain before
and it can drive you insane
if you choose to dwell
upon your hell

but today
and all the days going forward
i am going to be marching toward
that light
where i can see clearly
the energies about me
for what they be

and like these Notes from the Coffee Table
they are all
but expressions of me
and any damn possibilities
i choose to speak
in to life

notes from the Coffee Table # 24

Perhaps . . .
this is all
but a part of my purpose
the service of consciousness
. . . to be aware

i have experienced
first hand
my loneliness
my comfort
my joy
my despair
my power
my smiles
my tears
my hopes
my fears
and my love

am i the better for it ?

i will not judge,
but i have tasted
spaces in my self
i either
did not know
existed,
or have forgotten

and now,
here i most assuredly stand
and face my self
and the fact
that
these past days
since you have went away
i have expanded

and now
i understand

i understand why
you had to go
that you too
may get to know
your self

it is a solitudinous thing
and reconciliation
can not be accomplished
where conflict
and convolution
abides

we can not hide
from our selves
forever
as clever as we may be
nor can we
walk the path of life
with an uncertainty

we must remain diligent
in our vigilance
and be all seeking
and then perhaps,
just perhaps
we may catch a glimpse
a peeking into and
of the greater possibilities
life presents

as i dare look at the space
within
i become aware
and conscious
of my own exponentialness
and i am awestruck
with the construct
of creation
and it's perfect-ness

and . . .
i see you
and i
are the prefects
of a perfect expression
of the endlessness
born out of chaos
and that my dear soul
is the beauty manifest
we all possess

so in my penned confessions
in these
Notes from the Coffee Table
it becomes self evident
that we each are
so much more
than what we ever thought
our selves to be

and . . .
Life it's self
is calling for us
to explore this
road where an
unabashed bliss
awaits our arrival

so i thank you
for who you are

and in your doing so
the pursuing of you,
you were the catalyst
that spawned much of
my self

and this day
as i lay down these lines
in these Notes from the Coffee Table
i am in gratitude
for you

notes from the Coffee Table # 25

a very dear friend of mine
once wrote a Poem
which i have come to embrace
called
The Gift of Giving

within the Poem
there is a refrain
of consciousness
that speaks to me
speaks to this mind and spirit
i now express
and that is . . .
"Bless Them"

and this is my gift . .
i give

Notes from the Coffee Table . . .
reflective moments from when things change.

* The Gift if Giving : Justin Blackburn

addendum

oh,

a few words from Bill

In this addendum i have chosen to share with you, the Reader, a peek of my perspectives and the many faces of Love, Hope, Passion and Intimacy. For me personally it is of a Life Path Importance that i be authentic with my feelings no matter what gamut they may run emotionally. As in the body of this work 'Notes from the Coffee Table', as humans we do vary from Day to Day and Moment to Moment in our feelings and perspectives. Sometimes we express our Hopes, some times our Disdain. The important thing is we are expressing those things that move us through our Desire and our Hopes to our Expectations which allows us to face the Heart of our Humanity and possibly that Divine Particle which is a part of us all.

Blessed Be

bill

did i say i loved her

i don't quite remember
when she came into my life
it must have been that day
when i thought i was the sun
for her light was so intense
she brightened all that i was

where there was darkness
it fled
and i bled
naught but thoughts of goodness
whenever she crossed my mind
which was not often
because she was always on it

i think of the possibilities
of what lies on the road before me
and her
and the Stars begin to glisten
in the middle of the day
lighting my way
that my dreams
are seen
and i am redeemed
for she is all i ever needed

she speaks words to me
that move me
syllable by syllable
vowel by vowel
and her consonants
are constantly inspiring me
to want more of her
all of her
to taste her
hold her
kiss her
and i miss her
even when she
is right by my side

oh,
did i say i loved her

yes . . . i want

i want to whisper sweet things into your ear until they start to drip with honey and i want to watch as the sugar slowly crystallizes so i can suck on your lobes forever . . .ya ready ? . . . do you hear me ?

i want to visit your Holy Garden and plant deep kisses in your furrow that i may restructure your mind and your vocabulary so that the only three words you will ever utter again in your life are "Oh Bill mmmmmmmmmmm"

i want to lick your Desires of Divine Ecstasy until you want no more, for that is what i have come for, to make you my Vision, my Blissful Objective and i your Dream Master.

i want you to scream those three words i have taught you every time you blink your eyes for i am all you see . . . me, preparing you once again for that next step as you taste of this heaven where we become eternally fused and connected in the Communion of a Love that makes the Angels blush and God smile.

i want to teach you the Acrobatics of Love beyond understandings of possibilities, i want to teach you those positions that make the Kama Sutra blush deeply and run away and hide like the Kids Play it is.

i want you to hold my Head Softly, Delicately, Lovingly upon your Nipple Hardened Breast, where i rest in between every Breath and every Heartbeat, for you complete me as i complete you, for i am your life essence as you are mine.

i want to kneel before your Holy Fountain of Love and drink the warm liquid of your passions until i am filled with the Spirit of an Orgasmic Joy and Sweetness that was meant only for me . . . a place where i become the Universe and my eyes twinkle brighter than the Stars of all the Heavens created and those yet to come . . . i want to taste your Rainbows . . . let me be that one and only one who can drink from that Sacred place of thy Divine Essence and Beauty . . .

i want you to dance for me in your Dreams . . . in your Reality in your every cell . . every pore . . . every thought . . . listen to the music that is coming to you as i am coming for you . . . let us dance with a fervor that manifests our expectations into possibilities and thus into our reality . . let us loose our selves this day, this moment in the eternity of the happiness we were borne to experience .. . i want you to dance that dance upon my loins that urges me to release this liquid fire in your womb that we can birth a new truth to the Garden of Life that all may Drink, all may taste our Truth of what Love and Passion is . . let us dance the dance of smiles

and finally
i want you to be thankful for every wrong turn you have made upon the Road of life for it was those wrong turns that were the right turns, for they brought you to me, for i have been waiting for you a Lifetime . . . and the song of your heart you now sing makes Flowers Dance and Butterflies Smile and God pats Himself on the back as He says to Himself "Well Done"

yes . . . i want . . . You . . . what do you want ?

on the "Fair Ways" of Life

i met you upon the fair ways of life
the day was bright and bonny
we made acquaintance
we shared smiles
and "get to know you" conversation

we parted that day
but only for a while
for we made plans
to redress the address
of me knowing you
you knowing me

you see, it seemed
that love was perhaps getting a chance
to be redeemed
in our encounter

we spoke on the phone
and we shared our loneliness
as we decided
we no longer wished to hide
out from life
so we made a date
and God, just like you
i could not wait
so i invited you over

you came at 7
i was prepared
i was expecting heaven
and that is what i saw
when i opened
my door for you
damn you were beautiful
in all my blinded ways

but
little did i know
that the seed you had to sow
in my garden
was such a bitter fruit

you brought darkness
to my door
and you and your
convoluted disparaging angst
crossed my threshold
i felt it
yet still
i invited you in
cause i thought i needed you

we sat,
we talked,
we smiled the polite smiles . . .
we even laughed
and we . . .

and though the warning signs
were prevalent
i was lonely
and i needed someone
to touch
to hold
to share with
and hopefully
enfold
into my heart

so we pressed on
moved on
from 7:00 that evening
to the new dawn
to breakfast

it was all happening
so wonderfully fast

time skipped forward
and i thought
we were going toward
accomplishing
the vision of lovers
you know
that happily ever after
filled with love
and laughter

that was all i could think of
being loved
the right way
day and night

you were my objective
my fixation
the elation
of my dream come true . .
or should i say
the "we" in you and i
was where i wanted to be

you see,
i have been waiting
praying
anticipating
that this day would come
to my life
you know what i'm saying
i ain't playing
this shit was and is serious

and you came along
with your sweetness
your song
and i forgot who i am
who i was
cause
i was seriously delirious
furiously curious

like a man on a desert
i had desires
fires inside
that needed attending
i was broken
and i needed mending

but like so many other times
i put my trust
in the wrong things
i put it in you
instead of me

had i knew
we would come to this
i wonder now
would i have
sought that first kiss
that lead us down this road
while hoping for bliss
to ever be

damn i miss
the possibilities
of what could have been

but for me
like so many more of us
like i said
we trust in the wrong things
we trust in our head
our thinking
while slowly sinking
only to hold in disdain
the thoughts
that led us astray

many times i was aware
and there was a certain fear
that embraced my clarity
and the doubt and disparity
that loomed as a possibility
i would not have it
so i denied it
defied it
and now . .
i cry over it
shit !

the temporal delusions
were a happy place
with a happy face
yet in the end
the taste of the fruit
i now eat
is not sweet
nor replete
save for the lessons delivered

and i remember
those seemingly right turns
that i now see as wrong turns
and the road burns
along the way

but i must confess this
that even though
the bliss was an illusion
as is this confusion
i now speak about
i have no doubt
that i am the better for the experience
and for that i thank you
for through you
i have found another
piece of me
and hopefully i can learn to see
more of me
and less of that
glitz shit
on the "Fair Ways" of Life

ever for

my soul joyfully weeps in anticipation . . .
of your coming
...home.
i know with all due certainty
that you bear for me a bountiful heart,
filled with the gifts of "Heart",
with no limitations.

Through many restless nights
i rode the dream streams
of colorful light beams
looking over the horizons
of my aspirations . . .
looking for you

All my senses enlivened
with the urge but to be of you . . .
through you . . .
in you . . .
once again . . .
for you complete
the "me" of "me".

Over the eons
i have watched
the waxing and waning
of my passions and desires,
knowing that only your heart
could align my path with my truth.

Need i say that
the warm velvet of your ethereal touch
grounds me in the soil
of the garden of "Birth and Death"
exposing my silly illusions . . .
that i am finite.

Yes Love,
in my delusional haste to live
and the creations of my own hauntings,
i knew you were always there . . .
heart in hand
flowing with the essence of all life
. . . love,
for with Love,
Death willingly is trumped
and thus submits it's veil of deceit
to what "IS" . . . Life!

So, my dear
bring me the breath of "BE"ing that sustains us . . .
bring me the Joy Divine
bring me my Life's Light . . .
Light my Lantern once again
bring me our Life
that permeates all "BE"ing . . .
that i may awaken
and be transformed in the . . .

ever for.

when i think of you

i am missing touching you
as i did a million aeons ago
when we had wings

you seem so far away
though you are here with me
and i listen to the song of remembrance
as my Soul does sing

a billion light years apart
is nothing at all to me
for your luminescent loving beauty
still resides in my light within i see

no sorrow here my dear
nay, i shall never it embrace
for the grandeur of Love's beauty
is eternally etched upon your face

so, i thank you for the Fire
of inspire . . . ation
and the magnificence of elation
i feel
when i think of you

the resplendent joys of anticipation
have long over come any dismal thought
for you are all that i wished for
all i ever sought

so, i am dancing in the garden
where butterflies reflect their Holy sum
and i observe the movement of stillness
and the metamorphosis of goodness i become

like a child in the Cosmic Sandbox
i build Castles as i so deem
and with a Smile and Holy Tear
i actualize the Dream

when all of our essences'
is the all of what we be
as we shine brightly as one
energy, that all may clearly see

. . . when i think of you

i come to you

i have been searching for you for aeons
and your resonance has glowed within my soul
i have followed the flame
and the glow of your light
and it has directed me
through the presence of night

i come to you

sweet communion
was the order of the day
all i ever longed for was peace
a place where i may lay
my weary head
and rest

i draw my sword from it's scabbard for battle
and though i seek
to vanquish the enemy of the land
the enemy within
is the Demon
i wish to slay
this day

i see no other alternative
but to fight to my death
to give my life
to the higher order
of defending all that i love

yes i draw my sword
in accord
to a warriors duty
and honor

the odds are against
that any
of my comrades
will survive

i like these odds
for finally
i will be liberated
from this anguish
of being separated
all these aeons
from that which i need
you, the other half of my soul

i come to you

it was so many life times ago
i can vaguely remember
when you were banished
vanquished
from the court
for having my child

yes, we had defiled
the established dictums,
the rules of order
the modicum of behavior
for they said
you were beneath my stature
for i was of sovereign blood

i come to you

it is beginning
to come back to me now
my resonant memory
like the sun
shimmering upon the lake that day
when you taught me the way
and revealed unto me
the path
of a higher order
where borders
and restraints
to ones passions
no longer appeared
as real

i was feeling something
new that day
and i knew
that this journey
you led me on
was more than a simple quest
more than a test
more than but another conquest

it was a liberation of sorts
and the only retort
i could muster
was acquiescence
to the lesson before me

as the flower of a lighted consciousness
began to unfold
your flesh told stories
of a sweet bliss
found in but a single kiss
upon your lips
where my sensualities
became alive

and now in remembrance
of that which has transpired
so many lifetimes before
here i stand at the door
of a weariness of soul

and no thought any longer
can cajole me
to wish to proceed
in my search
for this flame
my twin
you, who makes me whole

yes i am tired
yet spirited
as a warrior should always be

and as i draw my sword
from its sheath
for the final time
there is a glimmer of light
reflections from the Sun
a glint
that catches my eye
that immobilizes
this fleeting introspective moment

and i remember
the shimmering
upon the lake that day
where i lay beside you
when you taught me the way
the path to a higher order
where borders
and restraints
to ones passions
no longer appeared
as real

and in solemn silence
i speak these words to you

i have been searching for you for aeons
and your resonance has glowed within my soul
i have followed the flame
and the glow of your light
has directed me
through the presence of my night

and this day
i come to you

~ * ~ come ~ * ~

come dance with me
and i will make beautiful love . . .
. . . to your soul
i will reach into your heart
and extract my palette
that i may paint your dreams
the colors of rainbows and butterflies

come walk with me
as we stroll by the stream
the stream of spiritual beauty
that abides within us both
we shall flow together
to the river, to the ocean
for we are one

come sing with me
the melodic tunes of bliss
where no cares exist
for we are the note
that harmonizes the world

come climb with me
as we explore the mountains . . .
. . . of our desires
peaking at the place
where passion overflows
into the skies beyond

come with me
give me your heart
in exchange for my own
and we shall dine . . .
. . . in the gardens
of divine joy

come my dear, come
for oneness is beckoning
come before the illusions . . .
. . . of time disappears
come my dear, come!

Come . . . response

Oh Beloved One of my Soul
i have been longing for your call
since the dawn of time
My heart weeps for your embrace
My dreams are of naught but thee
and . . . i . . . as one . . .
entwined, entangled and true
dancing across our clouds of joy
floating in a stream of color
that flows to the Oceans of all life
that we may give hope to the world
the hope that manifests
in to each Soul's reality . .

that Love is . . .
Love is
the breath of all things
Love is
the power that sustains
the dance of the Sun
across the skies of all existence
Love is
the soft night light of the Stars
and the Moon
that kisses mankind's aspirations

Yes my love, i am coming . . .
i hear your soft sweet whisperings
Yes my love i will take your hand,
as you take my heart
Feel my urgings for completion . . .
yes my love, i am here !

to live a life of Passion
blinds one from it's woes.

william s. peters, sr.

epilogue

William S. Peters, Sr.

about the Author

a biographical sketch of . . .

William S. Peters, Sr.

aka

'just bill'

Bill aka William S. Peters, Sr. was born in Philadelphia, Pennsylvania, April of Nineteen Hundred and Fifty One. He is the Proud Father of 11 children; 3 Sons and 8 Daughters and Grandfather of 8.

Bill's writing career spans a period quickly approaching 50 years. Being first Published in 1972, Bill has since went on to Author 22 additional Volumes of Poetry, Short Stories, etc., expressing his thoughts on matters of the Heart, Spirit, Consciousness and Humanity. His primary focus is that of Love, Peace and Understanding!

Due to his own personal circumstances that "Life's Travels" have presented to him such as the 'Crossing Over' of his Beloved Wife, Virisa on 2 July 2006, he says he found himself deeply immersed in an abysmal place filled with the convoluting voices of Love, Light, Darkness, Despair and Understanding. These Voices transmuted to feelings and thus to insights and thus to the expressive words you will find all over the internet and the pages of his extensive list of publications.

Bill is not only a Writer and Poet, he is also a Public Speaker, Empowerment Work Shop Leader, Consultant, Activist, Radio Personality, Broadcast Media Producer, Spoken Word and Recording Artist and so much more. Bill is the Founding Director of Inner Child Enterprises as well as the Past Director of Publicity for Society Hill Music. Bill has a Global Reading Audience and Fan Base. He is known for his Humanitarian Work and Activism in many communities in and outside of writing.

Bill has been featured in a variety magazines such as Big The Magazine, which incidentally he won the esteemed "Person of the Year Award" for the Year 2009 – 2010; Pen Strokes; Spoken Visions; Cattura; We are Creative People; Om Times and countless others. He has been featured on a plethora of Web Sites for his Insightful Spiritual Loving touch found in the words of his Expressions through Verse, Story, Commentary and Analogy.

As mentioned earlier, Bill is also a Spoken Word Artist and his current CD "*free thinker*" is available at his personal Web Site, www.iamjustbill.com as well as CD Baby, ReverbNation, Amazon, iTunes, etc.

He also founded the Inner Child Social Community, http://innerchild.ning.com. His Publicist, Adelle Banks Wilson of Adelle Conexxions and Manager, Michelle McKinnie, have nothing to say but good things about Bill and his Wonderful Empowering Spiritual Work. Bill is truly a blessing to anyone that is so graced to know him !

Bill is the Chief Executive of The Inner Child Radio Network which airs 7 Days a week on Blog Talk Radio and TalkShoe. For more information about all Inner Child Enterprises you can go to the Directory Web Site www.iaminnerchild.com. Bill's Goal with his work is simply to "Make a Difference"!

Bill additionally offers himself to others for Inspiration, Healing and Counseling. He has inspired, encouraged and supported many Light Workers, Healers, Writers, Poets and Artists to further their own expressive paths of *Self Empowerment*. He is also the Managing Director of a Unique Publishing Concern, where his primary focus is empowering Writers and assisting them in bringing their Words to Eyes and Ears of the General Populace.

Inner Child Enterprises, ltd.

Bill says . . .

I have always likened Life to that of a Garden. So, for me, Life is simply about the Seeds we Sow and Nourish. All things we "Think and Do", will "Be" Cause and eventually manifest itself to being an "Effect" within our own personal "Existences" and "Experiences" . . . whether it be Fruit, Flowers, Weeds or Barren Landscapes! Bill highly regards the Fruits of his Labor and wishes that everyone would thus go on to plant "Lovely" Seeds on "Good Ground" in their own Gardens of Life!

Namaste'

Janet P. Caldwell
Inner Child

Inner Child Links

http://www.iaminnerchild.com

http://www.innerchildpress.com

http://www.innerchild.ning.com

http://www.innerchildmagazine.com

http://www.youtube.com/user/krisar12

http://www.twitter.com/user/1innerchild

http://innerchildenterprises.blogspot.com

http://www.blogtalkradio.com/inner-child-radio

~

www.iamjustbill.com

http://www.facebook.com/billisthe1

some other books by Bill

All these Offerings and More are available

at

www.innerchildpress.com

or

www.iamjustbill.com

William S. Peters, Sr.

The
Vine
KeepeR
MESSAGES
IN POETRY & PROSE
William S. Peters, Sr.

This Too Shall Pass
a spiritual poetic journey
William S. Peters, Sr.

William S. Peters Sr. . . . . presents
the Wind . . .
the Mountain . . .
and the Sage . . .

the
light
in
the
window
whisperings from the soul of
William S. Peters, Sr.

Good Morning

my beloved Family

witticisms, greetings and early morning thoughts
From Bill's FaceBook Status

by

William S. Peters, Sr.

The Book of

by

William S. Peters, Sr.

my inner garden
by
William S. Peters, Sr.

Inner Child Press

Inner Child Press is a Publishing Company Founded and Operated by Writers. Our personal publishing experiences provides us an intimate understanding of the sometimes daunting challenges Writers, New and Seasoned may face in the Business of Publishing and Marketing their Creative "Written Work".

For more Information

Inner Child Press

www.innerchildpress.com

intouch@innerchildpress.com

~ fini ~

www.ingramcontent.com/pod-product-compliance
Lightning Source LLC
LaVergne TN
LVHW061224100826
845148LV00004B/848

9780615826370